CONTENTS

PRACTICAL VEDANTA

PART I

(Delivered in London, 10 November 1896)

I have been asked to say something about the practical position of the Vedanta philosophy. As I have told you, theory is very good indeed, but how are we to carry it into practice? If it be absolutely impracticable, no theory is of any value whatever, except as intellectual gymnastics. The Vedanta, therefore, as a religion must be intensely practical. We must be able to carry it out in every part of our lives. And not only this, the fictitious differentiation between religion and the life of the world must vanish, for the Vedanta teaches oneness — one life throughout. The ideals of religion must cover the whole field of life, they must enter into all our thoughts, and more and more into practice. I will enter gradually on the practical side as we proceed. But this series of lectures is intended to be a basis, and so we must first apply ourselves to theories and understand how they are worked out, proceeding from forest caves to busy streets and cities; and one peculiar feature we find is that many of these thoughts have been the outcome, not of retirement into forests, but have emanated from persons whom we expect to lead the busiest lives — from ruling monarchs.

Shvetaketu was the son of Aruni, a sage, most probably a recluse. He was brought up in the forest, but he went to the city of the Panchalas and appeared at the court of the king, Pravahana Jaivali. The king asked him, 'Do you know how beings depart hence at death?' 'No, sir.' 'Do you know how they return hither? 'No, sir.' 'Do you know the way of the fathers and the way of the gods?' 'No, sir.' Then the king asked other questions. Shvetaketu could not answer them. So the king told him that he knew nothing. The boy went back to his father, and the father admitted that he himself could not answer these questions. It was not that he was unwilling to answer these questions. It was not that he was unwilling to teach the boy, but he did not know these things. So he went to the king and asked to be taught these secrets. The king said that these things had been hitherto known only among kings; the priests never knew them. He, however, proceeded to teach him what he desired to know. In various Upanishads we find that this Vedanta philosophy is not the outcome of meditation in the forests only, but that the very best parts of it were thought out and expressed by brains which were busiest in the everyday affairs of life. We cannot conceive any man busier than an absolute monarch, a man who is ruling over millions of people, and yet, some of these rulers were deep thinkers.

Everything goes to show that this philosophy must be very practical; and later on, when we come to the Bhagavad-Gita—most of you, perhaps, have read it, it is the best commentary we have on the Vedanta philosophy—curiously enough the scene is laid on the battlefield, where Krishna teaches this philosophy to Arjuna; and the doctrine which stands out luminously in every page of the Gita is intense activity, but in the midst of it, eternal calmness. This is the secret of work, to attain which is the goal of the Vedanta. Inactivity, as we understand it in the sense of passivity, certainly cannot be the goal. Were it so, then the walls around us would be the most intelligent; they are inactive. Clods of earth, stumps of trees, would be the greatest sages in the world; they are inactive. Nor does inactivity become activity when it is combined with passion. Real activity, which is the goal of Vedanta, is combined with eternal calmness, the calmness which cannot be ruffled, the balance of mind which is never disturbed, whatever happens. And we all know from our experience in life that that is the best attitude for work.

I have been asked many times how we can work if we do not have the passion which we generally feel for work. I also thought in that way years ago, but as I am growing older, getting more experience, I find it is not true. The less passion there is, the better we work. The calmer we are, the better for us, and the more the amount of work we can do. When we let loose our feelings, we waste so much energy, shatter our nerves, disturb our minds, and accomplish very little work. The energy which ought to have gone out as work is spent as mere feeling, which counts for nothing. It is only when the mind is very calm and collected that the whole of its energy is spent in doing good work. And if you read the lives of the great workers which the world has produced, you will find that they were wonderfully calm men. Nothing, as it were, could throw them off their balance. That is why the man who becomes angry never does a great amount of work, and the man whom nothing can make angry accomplishes so much. The man who gives way to anger, or hatred, or any other passion, cannot work; he only breaks himself to pieces, and does nothing practical. It is the calm, forgiving, equable, well-balanced mind that does the greatest amount of work.

The Vedanta preaches the ideal; and the ideal, as we know, is always far ahead of the real, of the practical, as we may call it. There are two tendencies in human nature: one to harmonise the ideal with the life, and the other to elevate the life to the ideal. It is a great thing to understand this, for the former tendency is the temptation of our lives. I think that I can only do a certain class of work. Most of it, perhaps, is bad; most of it, perhaps, has a motive power of passion behind it, anger, or greed, or selfishness. Now if any man comes to preach to me a certain ideal, the first step towards which is to give up selfishness, to give up self-enjoyment, I think that is impractical. But when a man brings an ideal which can be reconciled with my selfishness, I am glad at once, and jump at it. That is the ideal for me. As the word 'orthodox' has been manipulated into various forms, so has been the word 'practical'. 'My doxy is orthodoxy; your doxy is heterodoxy.' So with practicality. What I think is practical, is to me the only practicality in the world. If I am a shopkeeper, I think shopkeeping the only practical pursuit in the world. If I am a thief, I think stealing is the best means of being practical; others are not practical. You see how we all use this word practical for things *we* like and can do. Therefore I will ask you to understand that Vedanta, though it is intensely practical, is always so in the sense of the ideal. It does not preach an impossible ideal, however high it be, and it is high enough for an ideal. In one word, this ideal is that you are divine, 'Thou art That'. This is the essence of Vedanta; after all its ramifications and intellectual gymnastics, you know the human soul to be pure and omniscient, you see that such superstitions as birth and death would be entire nonsense when spoken of in connection with the soul. The soul was never born and will never die, and all these ideas that we are going to die and are afraid to die are mere superstitions. And all such ideas as that we can do this, or cannot do that, are superstitions. We can do everything. The Vedanta teaches men to have faith in themselves first. As certain religions of the world say that a man who does not believe in a Personal God outside of himself is an atheist, so the Vedanta says, a man who does not believe in himself is an atheist. Not believing in the glory of our own soul is what the Vedanta calls atheism. To many this is, no doubt, a terrible idea; and most of us think that this ideal can never be reached; but the Vedanta insists that it can be realised by everyone. There is neither man nor woman nor child, nor difference of race or sex, nor anything that stands as a bar to the realisation of the ideal, because Vedanta shows that it is realised already, it is already there.

All the powers in the universe are already ours. It is we who have put our hands before our eyes and cry that it is dark. Know that there is no darkness around us. Take the hands away and there is the light which was from the beginning. Darkness never existed, weakness never existed. We who are fools cry that we are weak; we who are fools cry that we are impure. Thus Vedanta not only insists that the ideal is practical, but that it has been so all the time; and this Ideal, this Reality, is our own nature. Everything else that you see is false, untrue. As soon as you say, 'I am a little mortal being,' you are saying something which is not true, you are giving the lie to yourselves, you are hypnotising yourselves into something vile and weak and wretched.

The Vedanta recognises no sin, it only recognises error. And the greatest error, says the Vedanta, is to say that you are weak, that you are a sinner, a miserable creature, and that you have no power and you cannot do this and that. Every time you think in that way, you, as it were, rivet one more link in the chain that binds you down, you add one more layer of hypnotism on to your own soul. Therefore, whosoever thinks he is weak is wrong, whosoever thinks he is impure is wrong, and is throwing a bad thought into the world. This we must always bear in mind that in the Vedanta there is no attempt at reconciling the present life — the hypnotised life, this false life which we have assumed — with the ideal; but this false life must go, and the real life which is always existing must manifest itself, must shine out. No man becomes purer and purer, it is a matter of greater manifestation. The veil drops away, and the native purity of the soul begins to manifest itself. Everything is ours already — infinite purity, freedom, love, and power.

The Vedanta also says that not only can this be realised in the depths of forests or caves, but by men in all possible conditions of life. We have seen that the people who discovered these truths were neither living in caves nor forests, nor following the ordinary vocations of life, but men who, we have every reason to believe, led the busiest of lives, men who had to command armies, to sit on thrones, and look to the welfare of millions — and all these, in the days of absolute monarchy, and not as in these days when a king is to a great extent a mere figurehead. Yet they could find time to think out all these thoughts, to realise them, and to teach them to humanity. How much more then should it be practical for us whose lives, compared with theirs, are lives of leisure? That we cannot realise them is a shame to us, seeing that we are comparatively free all the time, having very little to do. My requirements are as nothing compared with those of an ancient absolute monarch. My wants are as nothing compared with the demands of Arjuna on the battlefield of Kurukshetra, commanding a huge army; and yet he could find time in the midst of the din and turmoil of battle to talk the highest philosophy and to carry it into his life also. Surely we ought to be able to do so as much in this life of ours — comparatively free, easy, and comfortable. Most of us here have more time than we think we have, if we really want to use it for good. With the amount of freedom we have we can attain to two hundred ideals in this life, if we will, but we must not degrade the ideal to the actual. One of the most insinuating things comes to us in the shape of persons who apologise for our mistakes and teach us how to make special excuses for all our foolish wants and foolish desires; and we think that their ideal is the only ideal we need have. But it is not so. The Vedanta teaches no such thing. The actual should be reconciled to the ideal, the present life should be made to coincide with life eternal.

For you must always remember that the one central ideal of Vedanta is this oneness. There are no two in anything, no two lives, nor even two different kinds of life for the two worlds. You will find the Vedas speaking of heavens and things like that at first; but later on, when they come to the highest ideals of their philosophy, they brush away all these things. There is but one life, one world, one existence. Everything is that One, the difference is in degree and not in kind. The difference between our lives is not in kind. The Vedanta entirely denies such ideas as that animals are separate from men, and that they were made and created by God to be used for our food.

Some people have been kind enough to start an anti-vivisection society. I asked a member, 'Why do you think, my friend, that it is quite lawful to kill animals for food, and not

to kill one or two for scientific experiments?'
He replied, 'Vivisection is most horrible, but
animals have been given to us for food.'
Oneness includes all animals. If man's life is
immortal, so also is the animal's. The
difference is only in degree and not in kind.
The amoeba and I are the same, the difference
is only in degree; and from the standpoint of
the highest life, all these differences vanish.
A man may see a great deal of difference
between grass and a little tree, but if you
mount very high, the grass and the biggest tree
will appear much the same. So, from the
standpoint of the highest ideal, the lowest
animal and the highest man are the same. If
you believe there is a God, the animals and the
highest creatures must be the same. A God
who is partial to his children called men, and
cruel to his children called brute beasts, is
worse than a demon. I would rather die a
hundred times than worship such a God. My
whole life would be a fight with such a God.
But there is no difference, and those who say
there is, are irresponsible, heartless people
who do not know. Here is a case of the word
practical used in a wrong sense. I myself may
not be a very strict vegetarian, but I
understand the ideal. When I eat meat I know
it is wrong. Even if I am bound to eat it under

certain circumstances, I know it is cruel. I must not drag my ideal down to the actual and apologise for my weak conduct in this way. The ideal is not to eat flesh, not to injure any being, for all animals are my brothers. If you can think of them as your brothers, you have made a little headway towards the brotherhood of all souls, not to speak of the brotherhood of man! That is child's play. You generally find that this is not very acceptable to many, because it teaches them to give up the actual, and go higher up to the ideal. But if you bring out a theory which is reconciled with their present conduct, they regard it as entirely practical.

There is this strongly conservative tendency in human nature; we do not like to move one step forward. I think of mankind just as I read of persons who become frozen in snow; all such, they say, want to go to sleep, and if you try to drag them up, they say, 'Let me sleep; it is so beautiful to sleep in the snow', and they die there in that sleep. So is our nature. That is what we are doing all our life, getting frozen from the feet upwards, and yet wanting to sleep. Therefore you must struggle towards the ideal, and if a man comes who wants to bring that ideal down to your level, and teach a religion that does not carry that highest ideal, do not listen to him. To me that is an impracticable religion. But if a man teaches a religion which presents the highest ideal, I am ready for him. Beware when anyone is trying to apologise for sense vanities and sense weaknesses. If anyone wants to preach that way to us, poor, sense-bound clods of earth as we have made ourselves by following that teaching, we shall never progress. I have seen many of these things, I have had some experience of the world, and my country is the land where religious sects grow like mushrooms. Every year new sects arise. But one thing I have marked, that it is only those that never want to reconcile the man of flesh with the man of truth that make progress. Wherever there is this false idea of reconciling fleshly vanities with the highest ideals, of dragging down God to the level of man, there comes decay. Man should not be degraded to worldly slavery, but should be raised up to God.

At the same time, there is another side to the question. We must not look down with contempt on others. All of us are going towards the same goal. The difference between weakness and strength is one of degree; the difference between virtue and vice is one of degree; the difference between heaven and hell is one of degree; the difference between life and death is one of degree; all differences in this world are of degree, and not of kind, because oneness is the secret of everything. All is One, which manifests Itself, either as thought, or life, or soul, or body, and the difference is only in degree. As such, we have no right to look down with contempt upon those who are not developed exactly in the same degree as we are. Condemn none; if you can stretch out a helping hand, do so. If you cannot, fold your hands, bless your brothers, and let them go their own way. Dragging down and condemning is not the way to work. Never is work accomplished in that way. We spend our energies in condemning others. Criticism and condemnation is a vain way of spending our energies, for in the long run we come to learn that all are seeing the same thing, are more or less approaching the same ideal, and that most of our differences are merely differences of expression.

Take the idea of sin. I was telling you just now the Vedantic idea of it, and the other idea is that man is a sinner. They are practically the same, only the one takes the positive and the other the negative side. One shows to man his strength and the other his weakness. There may be weakness, says the Vedanta, but never mind, we want to grow. Disease was found out as soon as man was born. Everyone knows his disease; it requires no one to tell us what our diseases are. But thinking all the time that we are diseased will not cure us — medicine is necessary. We may forget anything outside, we may try to become hypocrites to the external world, but in our heart of hearts we all know our weaknesses. But, says the Vedanta, being reminded of weakness does not help much; give strength, and strength does not come by thinking of weakness all the time. The remedy for weakness is not brooding over weakness, but thinking of strength. Teach men of the strength that is already within them. Instead of telling them they are sinners, the Vedanta takes the opposite position, and says, 'You are pure and perfect, and what you call sin does not belong to you.' Sins are very low degrees of Self-manifestation; manifest your Self in a high degree. That is the one thing to remember; all of us can do that. Never say, 'No', never say, 'I cannot', for you are infinite. Even time and space are as nothing compared with your nature. You can do anything and everything, you are almighty.

These are the principles of ethics, but we shall now come down lower and work out the details. We shall see how this Vedanta can be carried into our everyday life, the city life, the country life, the national life, and the home life of every nation. For, if a religion cannot help man wherever he may be, wherever he stands, it is not of much use; it will remain only a theory for the chosen few. Religion, to help mankind, must be ready and able to help him in whatever condition he is, in servitude or in freedom, in the depths of degradation or on the heights of purity; everywhere, equally, it should be able to come to his aid. The principles of Vedanta, or the ideal of religion, or whatever you may call it, will be fulfilled by its capacity for performing this great function.

The ideal of faith in ourselves is of the greatest help to us. If faith in ourselves had been more extensively taught and practised, I am sure a very large portion of the evils and miseries that we have would have vanished. Throughout the history of mankind, if any motive power has been more potent than another in the lives of all great men and women, it is that of faith in themselves. Born with the consciousness that they were to be great, they became great. Let a man go down as low as possible; there must come a time when out of sheer desperation he will take an upward curve and will learn to have faith in himself. But it is better for us that we should know it from the very first. Why should we have all these bitter experiences in order to gain faith in ourselves? We can see that all the difference between man and man is owing to the existence or non-existence of faith in himself. Faith in ourselves will do everything. I have experienced it in my own life, and am still doing so; and as I grow older that faith is becoming stronger and stronger. He is an atheist who does not believe in himself. The old religions said that he was an atheist who did not believe in God. The new religion says that he is the atheist who does not believe in himself. But it is not selfish faith, because the Vedanta, again, is the doctrine of oneness. It means faith in all, because you are all. Love for yourselves means love for all, love for animals, love for everything, for you are all one. It is the great faith which will make the world better. I am sure of that. He is the highest man who can say with truth, 'I know all about myself.' Do you know how much energy, how many powers, how many forces are still lurking behind that frame of yours? What scientist has known all that is in man? Millions of years have passed since man first came here, and yet but one infinitesimal part of his powers has been manifested. Therefore, you must not say that you are weak. How do you know what possibilities lie behind that degradation on the surface? You know but little of that which is within you. For behind you is the ocean of infinite power and blessedness.

'This Atman is first to be heard of.' Hear day and night that you are that Soul. Repeat it to yourselves day and night till it enters into your very veins, till it tingles in every drop of blood, till it is in your flesh and bone. Let the whole body be full of that one ideal, 'I am the birthless, the deathless, the blissful, the omniscient, the omnipotent, ever-glorious Soul.' Think on it day and night; think on it till it becomes part and parcel of your life. Meditate upon it, and out of that will come work. 'Out of the fullness of the heart the mouth speaketh,' and out of the fullness of the heart the hand worketh also. Action will come. Fill yourselves with the ideal; whatever you do, think well on it. All your actions will be magnified, transformed, deified by the very power of the thought. If matter is powerful, thought is omnipotent. Bring this thought to bear upon your life, fill yourselves with the thought of your almightiness, your majesty, and your glory. Would to God no superstitions had been put into your head! Would to God we had not been surrounded from our birth by all these superstitious influences and paralysing ideas of our weakness and vileness! Would to God that mankind had had an easier path through which to attain to the noblest and highest truths! But man had to pass through all this; do not make the path more difficult for those who are coming after you.

These are sometimes terrible doctrines to teach. I know people who get frightened at these ideas, but for those who want to be practical, this is the first thing to learn. Never tell yourselves or others that you are weak. Do good if you can, but do not injure the world. You know in your inmost heart that many of your limited ideas, this humbling of yourself and praying and weeping to imaginary beings are superstitions. Tell me one case where these prayers have been answered. All the answers that came were from your own hearts. You know there are no ghosts, but no sooner are you in the dark than you feel a little creepy sensation. That is so because in our childhood we have had all these fearful ideas put into our heads. But do not teach these things to others through fear of society and public opinion, through fear of incurring the hatred of friends, or for fear of losing cherished superstitions. Be masters of all these. What is there to be taught more in religion than the oneness of the universe and faith in one's self? All the works of mankind for thousands of years past have been towards this one goal, and mankind is yet working it out. It is your turn now and you already know the truth. For it has been taught on all sides. Not only philosophy and psychology, but materialistic sciences have declared it. Where is the scientific man today who fears to acknowledge the truth of this oneness of the universe? Who is there who dares talk of many worlds? All these are superstitions. There is only one life and one world, and this one life and one world is appearing to us as manifold. This manifoldness is like a dream. When you dream, one dream passes away and another comes. You do not live in your dreams. The dreams come one after another, scene after scene unfolds before you. So it is in this world of ninety per cent misery and ten per cent happiness. Perhaps after a while it will appear as ninety per cent happiness, and we shall call it' heaven, but a time comes to the sage when the whole thing vanishes, and this world appears as God Himself, and his own soul as God. It is not therefore that there are many worlds, it is not that there are many lives. All this manifoldness is the manifestation of that One. That One is manifesting Himself as many, as matter, spirit, mind, thought, and everything else. It is that One, manifesting Himself as many. Therefore the first step for us to take is to teach the truth to ourselves and to others.

Let the world resound with this ideal, and let superstitions vanish. Tell it to men who are weak and persist in telling it. You are the Pure One; awake and arise, O mighty one, this sleep does not become you. Awake and arise, it does not befit you. Think not that you are weak and miserable. Almighty, arise and awake, and manifest your own nature. It is not fitting that you think yourself a sinner. It is not fitting that you think yourself weak. Say that to the world, say it to yourselves, and see what a practical result comes, see how with an electric flash everything is manifested, how everything is changed. Tell that to mankind, and show them their power. Then we shall learn how to apply it in our daily lives.

To be able to use what we call Viveka (discrimination), to learn how in every moment of our lives, in every one of our actions, to discriminate between what is right and wrong, true and false, we shall have to know the test of truth, which is purity, oneness. Everything that makes for oneness is truth. Love is truth, and hatred is false, because hatred makes for multiplicity. It is hatred that separates man from man; therefore it is wrong and false. It is a disintegrating power; it separates and destroys.

Love binds, love makes for that oneness. You become one, the mother with the child, families with the city, the whole world becomes one with the animals. For love is Existence, God Himself; and all this is the manifestation of that One Love, more or less expressed. The difference is only in degree, but it is the manifestation of that One Love throughout. Therefore in all our actions we have to judge whether it is making for diversity or for oneness. If for diversity we have to give it up, but if it makes for oneness we are sure it is good. So with our thoughts; we have to decide whether they make for disintegration, multiplicity, or for oneness, binding soul to soul and bringing one influence to bear. If they do this, we will take them up, and if not, we will throw them off as criminal.

The whole idea of ethics is that it does not depend on anything unknowable, it does not teach anything unknown, but in the language of the Upanishad, 'The God whom you worship as an unknown God, the same I preach unto thee.' It is through the Self that you know anything. I see the chair; but to see the chair, I have first to perceive myself and

then the chair. It is in and through the Self that
the chair is perceived. It is in and through the
Self that you are known to me, that the whole
world is known to me; and therefore to say this
Self is unknown is sheer nonsense. Take off
the Self and the whole universe vanishes. In
and through the Self all knowledge comes.
Therefore, it is the best known of all. It is
yourself, that which you call I. You may
wonder how this I of me can be the I of you.
You may wonder how this limited I can be the
unlimited Infinite, but it is so. The limited is a
mere fiction. The Infinite has been covered
up, as it were, and a little of It is manifesting
as the I. Limitation can never come upon the
unlimited; it is a fiction. The Self is known,
therefore, to every one of us — man, woman, or
child — and even to animals. Without knowing
Him we can neither live nor move, nor have
our being; without knowing this Lord of all, we
cannot breathe or live a second. The God of
the Vedanta is the most known of all and is
not the outcome of imagination.

If this is not preaching a practical God, how
else could you teach a practical God? Where
is there a more practical God than He whom
I see before me, a God omnipresent — in every
being, more real than our senses? For you are
He, the Omnipresent God Almighty, the Soul

of your souls, and if I say you are not, I tell an untruth. I know it, whether at all times I realise it or not. He is the Oneness, the Unity of all, the Reality of all life and all existence.

These ideas of the ethics of Vedanta have to be worked out in detail, and, therefore, you must have patience. As I have told you, we want to take the subject in detail and work it up thoroughly, to see how the ideas grow from very low ideals, and how the one great Ideal of oneness has developed and become shaped into the universal love; and we ought to study these in order to avoid dangers. The world cannot find time to work it up from the lowest steps. But what is the use of our standing on higher steps if we cannot give the truth to others coming afterwards? Therefore, it is better to study it in all its workings; and first, it is absolutely necessary to clear the intellectual portion, although we know that intellectuality is almost nothing; for it is the heart that is of most importance. It is through the heart that the Lord is seen, and not through the intellect. The intellect is only the street-cleaner, cleansing the path for us, a secondary worker, the policeman; but the policeman is not a positive necessity for the workings of society. He is only to stop disturbances, to check wrong-doing, and that is all the work required of the intellect. When you read intellectual books, you think when you have mastered them, 'Bless the Lord that I am out of them', because the intellect is blind and cannot move of itself, it has neither hands nor feet. It is feeling that works, that moves with speed infinitely superior to that of electricity or anything else. Do you feel? — that is the question. If you do, you will see the Lord: It is the feeling that you have today that will be intensified, deified, raised to the highest platform, until it feels everything, the oneness in everything, till it feels God in itself and in others. The intellect can never do that. 'Different methods of speaking words, different methods of explaining the texts of books, these are for the enjoyment of the learned, not for the salvation of the soul' (*Vivekachudamani*, 58).

Those of you who have read Thomas a Kempis know how in every page he insists on this, and almost every holy man in the world has insisted on it. Intellect is necessary, for without it we fall into crude errors and make all sorts of mistakes. Intellect checks these; but beyond that, do not try to build anything upon it. It is an inactive, secondary help; the real help is feeling, love. Do you feel for others? If you do, you are growing in oneness.

If you do not feel for others, you may be the most intellectual giant ever born, but you will be nothing; you are but dry intellect, and you will remain so. And if you feel, even if you cannot read any book and do not know any language, you are in the right way. The Lord is yours.

Do you not know from the history of the world where the power of the prophets lay? Where was it? In the intellect? Did any of them write a fine book on philosophy, on the most intricate ratiocinations of logic? Not one of them. They only spoke a few words. Feel like Christ and you will be a Christ; feel like Buddha and you will be a Buddha. It is feeling that is the life, the strength, the vitality, without which no amount of intellectual activity can reach God. Intellect is like limbs without the power of locomotion. It is only when feeling enters and gives them motion that they move and work on others. That is so all over the world, and it is a thing which you must always remember. It is one of the most practical things in Vedantic morality, for it is the teaching of the Vedanta that you are all prophets, and all must be prophets. The book is not the proof of your conduct, but you are the proof of the book. How do you know that a book teaches truth? Because you are truth and feel it. That is what the Vedanta says. What is the proof of the Christs and the Buddhas of the world? That you and I feel like them. That is how you and I understand that they were true. Our prophet-soul is the proof of their prophet-soul. Your godhead is the proof of God Himself. If you are not a prophet, there never has been anything true of God. If you are not God, there never was any God, and never will be. This, says the Vedanta, is the ideal to follow. Everyone of us will have to become a prophet, and you are that already. Only *know* it. Never think there is anything impossible for the soul. It is the greatest heresy to think so. If there is sin, this is the only sin — to say that you are weak, or others are weak.

PRACTICAL VEDANTA

PART II

(Delivered in London, 12 November 1896)

I will relate to you a very ancient story from the Chhandogya Upanishad, which tells how knowledge came to a boy. The form of the story is very crude, but we shall find that it contains a principle. A young boy said to his mother, 'I am going to study the Vedas. Tell me the name of my father and my caste.' The mother was not a married woman, and in India the child of a woman who has not been married is considered an outcast; he is not recognised by society and is not entitled to study the Vedas. So the poor mother said, 'My child, I do not know your family name; I was in service, and served in different places; I do not know who your father is , but my name is Jabala and your name is Satyakama.' The little child went to a sage and asked to be taken as a student. The sage asked him, 'What is the name of your father, and what is your caste?' The boy repeated to him what he had heard from his mother. The sage at once said, 'None but a Brahmana could speak such a damaging truth about himself. You are a Brahmana and I will teach you. You have not swerved from truth.' So he kept the boy with him and educated him.

Now come some of the peculiar methods of education in ancient India. This teacher gave Satyakama four hundred lean, weak cows to take care of, and sent him to the forest. There he went and lived for some time. The teacher had hold him to come back when the herd would increase to the number of one thousand. After a few years, one day Satyakama heard a big bull in the herd saying to him, 'We are a thousand now; take us back to your teacher. I will teach you a little of Brahman.' 'Say on, sir,' said Satyakama. Then the bull said, 'The East is a part of the Lord, so is the West, so is the South, so is the North. The four cardinal points are the four parts of Brahman. Fire will also teach you something of Brahman.' Fire was a great symbol in those days, and every student had to procure fire and make offerings. So on the following day, Satyakama started for his Guru's house, and when in the evening he had performed his oblation, and worshipped at the fire, and was sitting near it, he heard a voice come from the fire, 'O Satyakama.' 'Speak, Lord,' said

Satyakama. (Perhaps you may remember a very similar story in the Old Testament, how Samuel heard a mysterious voice.) 'O Satyakama, I am come to teach you a little of Brahman. This earth is a portion of that Brahman. The sky and the heaven are portions of It. The ocean is a part of that Brahman.' Then the fire said that a certain bird would also teach him something. Satyakama continued his journey and on the next day when he had performed his evening sacrifice a swan came to him and said, 'I will teach you something about Brahman. This fire which you worship, O Satyakama, is a part of that Brahman. The sun is a part, the moon is a part, the lightning is a part of that Brahman. A bird called Madgu will tell you more about it.' The next evening that bird came, and a similar voice was heard by Satyakama, 'I will tell you something about Brahman. Breath is a part of Brahman, sight is a part, hearing is a part, the mind is a part.' Then the boy arrived at his teacher's place and presented himself before him with due reverence. No sooner had the teacher seen this disciple than he remarked: 'Satyakama, thy face shines like that of a knower of Brahman! Who then has taught thee?' 'Beings other than men,' replied Satyakama. 'But I wish that you should teach me, sir. For I have heard from men like you that knowledge which is learnt from a Guru alone leads to the supreme good.' Then the sage taught him the same knowledge which he had received from the gods. 'And nothing was left out, yea, nothing was left out.'

Now, apart from the allegories of what the bull, the fire, and the birds taught, we see the tendency of the thought and the direction in which it was going in those days. The great idea of which we here see the germ is that all these voices are inside ourselves. As we understand these truths better, we find that the voice is in our own heart, and the student understood that all the time he was hearing the truth; but his explanation was not correct. He was interpreting the voice as coming from the external world, while all the time, it was within him. The second idea that we get is that of making the knowledge of the Brahman practical. The world is always seeking the practical possibilities of religion, and we find in these stories how it was becoming more and more practical every day. The truth was shown through everything with which the students were familiar. The fire they were worshipping was Brahman, the earth was a part of Brahman, and so on.

The next story belongs to Upakosala

Kamalayana, a disciple of this Satyakama, who went to be taught by him and dwelt with him for some time. Now Satyakama went away on a journey, and the student became very downhearted; and when the teacher's wife came and asked him why he was not eating, the boy said, 'I am too unhappy to eat.' Then a voice came from the fire he was worshipping, saying 'This life is Brahman, Brahman is the ether, and Brahman is happiness. Know Brahman.' 'I know, sir,' the boy replied, 'that life is Brahman, but that It is ether and happiness I do not know.' Then it explained that the two words ether and happiness signified one thing in reality, viz the sentient ether (pure intelligence) that resides in the heart. So, it taught him Brahman as life and as the ether in the heart. Then the fire taught him, 'This earth, food, fire, and sun whom you worship, are forms of Brahman. The person that is seen in the sun, I am He. He who knows this and meditates on Him, all his sins vanish and he has long life and becomes happy. He who lives in the cardinal points, the moon, the stars, and the water, I am He. He who lives in this life, the ether, the heavens, and the lightning, I am He.' Here too we see the same idea of practical religion. The things which they were worshipping, such as the fire, the sun, the moon, and so forth, and the voice with which they were familiar, form the subject of the stories which explain them and give them a higher meaning. And this is the real, practical side of Vedanta. It does not destroy the world, but it explains it; it does not destroy the person, but explains him; it does not destroy the individuality, but explains it by showing the real individuality. It does not show that this world is vain and does not exist, but it says, 'Understand what this world is, so that it may not hurt you.' The voice did not say to Upakosala that the fire which he was worshipping, or the sun, or the moon, or the lightning, or anything else, was all wrong, but it showed him that the same spirit which was inside the sun, and moon, and lightning, and the fire, and the earth, was in him, so that everything became transformed, as it were, in the eyes of Upakosala. The fire which was merely a material fire before, in which to make oblations, assumed a new aspect and became the Lord. The earth became transformed, life became transformed, the sun, the moon, the stars, the lightning, everything became transformed and deified. Their real nature was known. The theme of the Vedanta is to see the Lord in everything, to see things in their real nature, not as they appear to be. Then another lesson is taught in the Upanishads: 'He who shines through the eyes is Brahman; He is the Beautiful One, He is the Shining One. He shines in all these worlds.' A certain peculiar light, a commentator says, which comes to the pure man, is what is meant by the light in the eyes, and it is said that when a man is pure such a light will shine in his eyes, and that light belongs really to the Soul within, which is everywhere. It is the same light which shines in the planets, in the stars, and suns.

I will now read to you some other doctrine of these ancient Upanishads, about birth and death and so on. Perhaps it will interest you. Shvetaketu went to the king of the Panchalas, and the king asked him, 'Do you know where people go when they die? Do you know how they come back? Do you know why the other world does not become full?' The boy replied that he did not know. Then he went to his father and asked him the same questions. The father said, 'I do not know,' and he went to the king. The king said that this knowledge was never known to the priests, it was only with the kings, and that was the reason why kings ruled the world. This man stayed with the king for some time, for the king said he would teach him. 'The other world, O Gautama, is the fire. The sun is its fuel. The rays are the smoke. The day is the flame. The moon is the embers. And the stars are the sparks. In this fire the gods pour libation of faith and from this libation king Soma is born.' So on he goes. 'You need not make oblation to that little fire: the whole world is that fire, and this oblation, this worship, is continually going on. The gods, and the angels, and everybody is worshipping it. Man is the greatest symbol of fire, the body of man.' Here also we see the ideal becoming practical and Brahman is seen in everything. The principle that underlies all these stories is that invented symbolism may be good and helpful, but already better symbols exist than any we can invent. You may invent an image through which to worship God, but a better image already exists, the living man. You may build a temple in which to worship God, and that may be good, but a better one, a much higher one, already exists, the human body.

You remember that the Vedas have two parts, the ceremonial and the knowledge portions. In time ceremonials had multiplied and become so intricate that it was almost hopeless to disentangle them, and so in the Upanishads we find that the ceremonials are almost done away with, but gently, by explaining them. We see that in old times they had these oblations and sacrifices, then the philosophers came, and instead of snatching away the symbols from the hands of the ignorant, instead of taking the negative position, which we unfortunately find so general in modern reforms, they gave them something to take their place. 'Here is the symbol of fire,' they said. 'Very good! But here is another symbol, the earth. What a grand, great symbol! Here is this little temple, but the whole universe is a temple; a man can worship anywhere. There are the peculiar figures that men draw on the earth, and there are the altars, but here is the greatest of altars, the living, conscious human body, and to worship at this altar is far higher than the worship of any dead symbols.'

We now come to a peculiar doctrine. I do not understand much of it myself. If you can make something out of it, I will read it to you. When a man dies, who has by meditation purified himself, and got knowledge, he first goes to light, then from light to day, from day to the light half of the moon, from that to the six months when the sun goes to the north, from that to the year, from the year to the sun, from the sun to the moon, from the moon to the lightning, and when he comes to the sphere of lightning, he meets a person who is not human, and that person leads him to (the conditioned) Brahman. This is the way of the gods. When sages and wise persons die, they go that way and they do not return. What is meant by this month and year, and all these things, no one understands clearly. Each one gives his own meaning, and some say it is all nonsense. What is meant by going to the world of the moon and of the sun, and this person who comes to help the soul after it has reached the sphere of lightning, no one knows. There is an idea among the Hindus that the moon is a place where life exists, and we shall see how life has come from there. Those that have not attained to knowledge, but have done good work in this life, first go, when they die, through smoke, then to night, then to the dark fifteen days, then to the six months when the sun goes to the south, and from that they go to the region of their forefathers, then to ether, then to the region of the moon, and there become the food of the gods, and later, are born as gods and live there so long as their good works will permit. And when the effect of the good work has been finished, they come back to earth by the same route. They first become ether, and then air, and then smoke, and then mist, then cloud, and then fall upon the earth as raindrops; then they get into food, which is eaten up by human beings, and finally become their children. Those whose works have been very good take birth in good families, and those whose works have been bad take bad births, even in animal bodies. Animals are continually coming to and going from this earth. That is why the earth is neither full nor empty.

Several ideas we can get also from this, and later on, perhaps, we shall be able to understand it better, and we can speculate a little upon what it means. The last part which deals with how those who have been in heaven return, is clearer, perhaps, than the first part; but the whole idea seems to be this, that there is no permanent heaven without realising God. Now some people who have not realised God, but have done good work in this world, with the view of enjoying the results, go, when they die, through this and that place, until they reach heaven, and there they are born in the same way as we are here, as children of the gods, and they live there as long as their good works will permit. Out of this comes one basic idea of the Vedanta that everything which has name and form is transient. This earth is transient, because it has name and form, and so the heavens must be transient, because there also name and form remain. A heaven which is eternal will be contradictory in terms, because everything that has name and form must begin in time, exist in time, and end in time. These are settled doctrines of the Vedanta, and as such the heavens are given up.

We have seen in the Samhita that the idea of heaven was that it was eternal, much the same as is prevalent among Mohammedans and Christians. The Mohammedans concretise it a little more. They say it is a place where there are gardens, beneath which rivers run. In the desert of Arabia water is very desirable, so the Mohammedan always conceives of his heaven as containing much water. I was born in a country where there are six months of rain every year. I should think of heaven, I suppose, as a dry place, and so also would the English people. These heavens in the Samhita are eternal, and the departed have beautiful bodies and live with their forefathers, and are happy ever afterwards. There they meet with their parents, children, and other relatives, and lead very much the same sort of life as here, only much happier. All the difficulties and obstructions to happiness in this life have vanished, and only its good parts and enjoyments remain. But however comfortable mankind may consider this state of things, truth is one thing and comfort is another. There are cases where truth is not comfortable until we reach its climax. Human nature is very conservative. It does something, and having once done that, finds it hard to get out of it. The mind will not receive new thoughts, because they bring discomfort.

In the Upanishads, we see a tremendous departure made. It is declared that these heavens in which men live with the ancestors after death cannot be permanent, seeing that everything which has name and form must die. If there are heavens with forms, these heavens must vanish in course of time; they may last millions of years, but there must come a time when they will have to go. With this idea came another that these souls must come back to earth, and that heavens are places where they enjoy the results of their good works, and after these effects are finished they come back into this earth-life again. One thing is clear from this that mankind had a perception of the philosophy of causation even at the early time. Later on we shall see how our philosophers bring that out in the language of philosophy and logic, but here it is almost in the language of children. One thing you may remark in reading these books, that it is all internal perception. If you ask me if this can be practical, my answer is, it has been practical first, and philosophical next. You can see that first these things have been perceived and realised and then written. This world spoke to the early thinkers. Birds spoke to them, animals spoke to them, the sun and the moon spoke to them; and little by little they realised things, and got into the heart of nature. Not by cogitation, not by the force of logic, not by picking the brains of others and making a big book, as is the fashion in modern times, not even as I do, by taking up one of their writings and making a long lecture, but by patient investigation and discovery they found out the truth. Its essential method was practice, and so it must be always. Religion is ever a practical science, and there never was nor will be any theological religion. It is practice first, and knowledge afterwards. The idea that souls come back is already there. Those persons who do good work with the idea of a result, get it, but the result is not permanent. There we get the idea of causation very beautifully put forward, that the effect is only commensurate with the cause. As the cause is, so the effect will be. The cause being finite, the effect must be finite. If the cause is eternal the effect can be eternal, but all these causes, doing good work, and all other things, are only finite causes, and as such cannot produce infinite result.

We now come to the other side of the question. As there cannot be an eternal heaven, on the same grounds, there cannot be an eternal hell. Suppose I am a very wicked man, doing evil every minute of my life. Still, my whole life here, compared with my eternal life, is nothing. If there be an eternal punishment, it will mean that there is an infinite effect produced by a finite cause, which cannot be. If I do good all my life, I cannot have an infinite heaven; it would be making the same mistake. But there is a third course which applies to those who have known the Truth, to those who have realised It. This is the only way to get beyond this veil of Maya — to realise what Truth is; and the Upanishads indicate what is meant by realising the Truth.

It means recognising neither good nor bad, but knowing all as coming from the Self; Self is in everything. It means denying the universe; shutting your eyes to it; seeing the Lord in hell as well as in heaven; seeing the Lord in death as well as in life. This is the line of thought in the passage I have read to you; the earth is a symbol of the Lord, the sky is the Lord, the place we fill is the Lord, everything is Brahman. And this is to be seen, realised, not simply talked or thought about. We can see as its logical consequence that when the soul has realised that everything is full of the Lord, of Brahman, it will not care whether it goes to heaven, or hell, or anywhere else; whether it be born again on this earth or in heaven. These things have ceased to have any meaning to that soul, because every place is the same, every place is the temple of the Lord, every place has become holy, and the presence of the Lord is all that it sees in heaven, or hell, or anywhere else. Neither good nor bad, neither life nor death — only the one infinite Brahman exists.

According to the Vedanta, when a man has arrived at that perception, he has become free, and he is the only man who is fit to live in this world. Others are not. The man who sees evil, how can he live in this world? His life is a mass of misery. The man who sees dangers, his life is a misery; the man who sees death, his life is a misery. That man alone can live in this world, he alone can say, 'I enjoy this life, and I am happy in this life', who has seen the Truth, and the Truth in everything. By the by, I may tell you that the idea of hell does not occur in the Vedas anywhere. It comes with the Puranas much later. The worst punishment according to the Vedas is coming back to earth, having another chance in this world. From the very first we see the idea is taking the impersonal turn. The ideas of punishment and reward are very material, and they are only consonant with the idea of a human God, who loves one and hates another, just as we do. Punishment and reward are only admissible with the existence of such a God. They had such a God in the Samhita, and there we find the idea of fear entering, but as soon as we come to the Upanishads, the idea of fear vanishes, and the impersonal idea takes its place. It is naturally the hardest thing for man to understand, this impersonal idea, for he is always clinging on to the person. Even people who are thought to be great thinkers get disgusted at the idea of the Impersonal God. But to me it seems so absurd to think of God as an embodied man. Which is the higher idea, a living God, or a dead God? A God whom nobody sees, nobody knows, or a God known?

The Impersonal God is a living God, a principle. The difference between personal and impersonal is this, that the personal is only a man, and the impersonal idea is that He is the angel, the man, the animal, and yet something more which we cannot see, because Impersonality includes all personalities, is the sum total of everything in the universe, and infinitely more besides. 'As the one fire coming into the world is manifesting itself in so many forms, and yet is infinitely more besides', so is the Impersonal.

We want to worship a living God. I have seen nothing but God all my life, nor have you. To see this chair you first see God, and then the chair in and through Him. He is everywhere saying, 'I am'. The moment you feel 'I am', you are conscious of Existence. Where shall we go to find God if we cannot see Him in our own hearts and in every living being? 'Thou art the man, Thou art the woman, Thou art the girl, and Thou art the boy. Thou art the old man tottering with a stick. Thou art the young man walking in the pride of his strength.' Thou art all that exists, a wonderful living God who is the only fact in the universe. This seems to many to be a terrible contradiction to the traditional God who lives behind a veil somewhere and whom nobody ever sees. The priests only give us an assurance that if we follow them, listen to their admonitions, and walk in the way they mark out for us — then when we die, they will give us a passport to enable us to see the face of God! What are all these heaven ideas but simply modifications of this nonsensical priestcraft?

Of course the Impersonal idea is very destructive; it takes away all trade from the priests, churches, and temples. In India there

is a famine now, but there are temples in each
one of which there are jewels worth a king's
ransom! If the priests taught this Impersonal
idea to the people, their occupation would be
gone. Yet we have to teach it unselfishly,
without priestcraft. You are God and so am I;
who obeys whom? Who worships whom? You
are the highest temple of God; I would rather
worship you than any temple, image, or Bible.
Why are some people so contradictory in their
thought? They are like fish slipping through
our fingers. They say they are hard-headed
practical men. Very good. But what is more
practical than worshipping here, worshipping
you? I see you, feel you, and I know you are
God. The Mohammedan says, there is no God
but Allah. The Vedanta says, there is nothing
that is not God. It may frighten many of you,
but you will understand it by degrees. The
living God is within you, and yet you are
building churches and temples and believing
all sorts of imaginary nonsense. The only God
to worship is the human soul in the human
body. Of course all animals are temples too,
but man is the highest, the Taj Mahal of
temples. If I cannot worship in that, no other
temple will be of any advantage. The moment
I have realised God sitting in the temple of
every human body, the moment I stand in

reverence before every human being and see God in him — that moment I am free from bondage, everything that binds vanishes, and I am free.

This is the most practical of all worship. It has nothing to do with theorising and speculation, yet it frightens many. They say it is not right. They go on theorising about old ideals told them by their grandfathers, that a God somewhere in heaven had told some one that he was God. Since that time we have only theories. This is practicality according to them, and our ideas are impractical! No doubt, the Vedanta says that each one must have his own path, but the path is not the goal. The worship of a God in heaven and all these things are not bad, but they are only steps towards the Truth and not the Truth itself. They are good and beautiful, and some wonderful ideas are there, but the Vedanta says at every point, 'My friend, Him whom you are worshipping as unknown, I worship as thee. He whom you are worshipping as unknown and are seeking for, throughout the universe, has been with you all the time. You are living through Him, and He is the Eternal Witness of the universe.' 'He whom all the Vedas worship, nay, more, He who is always present in the eternal "I", He existing, the whole universe exists. He is the light and life of the universe. If the "I" were not in you, you would not see the sun, everything would be a dark mass. He shining, you see the world.'

One question is generally asked, and it is this that this may lead to a tremendous amount of difficulty. Everyone of us will think, 'I am God, and whatever I do or think must be good, for God can do no evil.' In the first place, even taking this danger of misinterpretation for granted, can it be proved that on the other side the same danger does not exist? They have been worshipping a God in heaven separate from them, and of whom they are much afraid. They have been born shaking with fear, and all their life they will go on shaking. Has the world been made much better by this? Those who have understood and worshipped a Personal God, and those who have understood and worshipped an Impersonal God, on which side have been the great workers of the world — gigantic workers, gigantic moral powers? Certainly on the Impersonal. How can you expect morality to be developed through fear? It can never be. 'Where one sees another, where one hears another, that is Maya. When one does not see another, when one does not hear another, when everything has become the Atman, who sees whom, who perceives whom?' It is all He, and all I, at the same time. The soul has become pure. Then, and then alone we understand what love is. Love cannot come through fear, its basis is freedom. When we really begin to love the world, then we understand what is meant by brotherhood of mankind, and not before.

So, it is not right to say that the Impersonal idea will lead to a tremendous amount of evil in the world, as if the other doctrine never lent itself to works of evil, as if it did not lead to sectarianism deluging the world with blood and causing men to tear each other to pieces. 'My God is the greatest God, let us decide it by a free fight.' That is the outcome of dualism all over the world. Come out into the broad open light of day, come out from the little narrow paths, for how can the infinite soul rest content to live and die in small ruts? Come out into the universe of Light. Everything in the universe is yours, stretch out your arms and embrace it with love. If you ever felt you wanted to do that, you have felt God.

You remember that passage in the sermon of Buddha, how he sent a thought of love towards the south, the north, the east, and the west, above and below, until the whole universe was filled with this love, so grand, great, and infinite. When you have that feeling, you have true personality. The whole universe is one person; let go the little things. Give up the small for the Infinite, give up small enjoyments for infinite bliss. It is all yours, for the Impersonal includes the Personal. So God is Personal and Impersonal at the same time. And Man, the Infinite, Impersonal Man, is manifesting Himself as person. We the infinite have limited ourselves, as it were, into small parts. The Vedanta says that Infinity is our true nature; it will never vanish, it will abide for ever. But we are limiting ourselves by our Karma, which like a chain round our necks has dragged us into this limitation. Break that chain and be free. Trample law under your feet. There is no law in human nature, there is no destiny, no fate. How can there be law in infinity? Freedom is its watchword. Freedom is its nature, its birthright. Be free, and then have any number of personalities you like. Then we will play like the actor who comes upon the stage and plays the part of a beggar. Contrast him with the actual beggar walking in the streets. The scene is perhaps, the same in both cases, the words, are perhaps, the same, but yet what difference! The one enjoys his beggary, while the other is suffering misery from it. And what makes this difference? The one is free and the other is bound. The actor knows his beggary is not true, but that he has assumed it for play, while the real beggar thinks that it is his too familiar state and that he has to bear it whether he wills it or not. This is the law. So long as we have no knowledge of our real nature, we are beggars, jostled about by every force in nature; and made slaves of by everything in nature; we cry all over the world for help, but help never comes to us; we cry to imaginary beings, and yet it never comes. But still we hope help will come, and thus in weeping, wailing, and hoping, one life is passed, and the same play goes on and on.

Be free; hope for nothing from anyone. I am sure if you look back upon your lives you will find that you were always vainly trying to get help from others which never came. All the help that has come was from within yourselves. You only had the fruits of what you yourselves worked for, and yet you were strangely hoping all the time for help. A rich man's parlour is always full; but if you notice, you do not find the same people there. The visitors are always hoping that they will get something from those wealthy men, but they never do. So are our lives spent in hoping, hoping, hoping, which never comes to an end. Give up hope, says the Vedanta. Why should you hope? You *have* everything, nay you are everything. What are you hoping for? If a king goes mad, and runs about trying to find the king of his country, he will never find him, because he is the king himself. He may go through every village and city in his own country, seeking in every house, weeping and wailing, but he will never find him, because he is the king himself. It is better that we know we are God and give up this fool's search after Him; and knowing that we are God we become happy and contented. Give up all these mad pursuits, and then play your part in the universe, as an actor on the stage.

The whole vision is changed, and instead of an eternal prison this world has become a playground; instead of a land of competition it is a land of bliss, where there is perpetual spring, flowers bloom and butterflies flit about. This very world becomes heaven, which formerly was hell. To the eyes of the bound it is a tremendous place of torment, but to the eyes of the free it is quite otherwise. This one life is the universal life, heavens and all those places are here. All the gods are here, the prototypes of man. The gods did not create man after their type, but man created gods. And here are the prototypes, here is Indra, here is Varuna, and all the gods of the universe. We have been projecting our little doubles, and we are the originals of these gods, we are the real, the only gods to be worshipped. This is the view of the Vedanta, and this its practicality. When we have become free, we need not go mad and throw up society and rush off to die in the forest or the cave; we shall remain where we were, only we shall understand the whole thing. The same phenomena will remain, but with a new meaning. We do not know the world yet; it is only through freedom that we see what it is, and understand its nature. We shall see then that this so-called law, or fate, or destiny occupied only an infinitesimal part of our nature. It was only one side, but on the other side there was freedom all the time. We did not know this, and that is why we have been trying to save ourselves from evil by hiding our faces in the ground, like the hunted hare. Through delusion we have been trying to forget our nature, and yet we could not; it was always calling upon us, and all our search after God or gods, or external freedom, was a search after our real nature. We mistook the voice. We thought it was from the fire, or from a god or the sun, or moon, or stars, but at last we have found that it was from within ourselves. Within ourselves is this eternal voice speaking of eternal freedom; its music is eternally going on. Part of this music of the Soul has become the earth, the law, this universe, but it was always ours and always will be. In one word, the ideal of Vedanta is to know man as he really is, and this is its message, that if you cannot worship your brother man, the manifested God, how can you worship a God who is unmanifested?

Do you not remember what the Bible says, 'If you cannot love your brother whom you have seen, how can you love God whom you have not seen?' If you cannot see God in the human face, how can you see Him in the clouds, or in images made of dull, dead matter, or in mere fictitious stories of our brain? I shall call you religious from the day you begin to see God in men and women, and then you will understand what is meant by turning the left cheek to the man who strikes you on the right. When you see man as God, everything, even the tiger, will be welcome. Whatever comes to you is but the Lord, the Eternal, the Blessed One, appearing to us in various forms, as our father, and mother, and friend, and child— they are our own soul playing with us.

As our human relationships can thus be made divine, so our relationship with God may take any of these forms and we can look upon Him as our father, or mother, or friend, or beloved. Calling God Mother is a higher ideal than calling Him Father; and to call Him Friend is still higher; but the highest is to regard Him as the Beloved. The highest point of all is to see no difference between lover and beloved. You may remember, perhaps, the old Persian story, of how a lover came and knocked at the door of the beloved and was asked, 'Who are you?' He answered, 'It is I', and there was no response. A second time he came, and exclaimed, 'I am here', but the door was not opened. The third time he came, and the voice asked from inside, 'Who is there?' He replied, 'I am thyself, my beloved', and the door opened. So is the relation between God and ourselves. He is in everything, He is everything. Every man and woman is the palpable, blissful, living God. Who says God is unknown? Who says He is to be searched after? We have found God eternally. We have been living in Him eternally; everywhere He is eternally known, eternally worshipped.

Then comes another idea, that other forms of worship are not errors. This is one of the great points to be remembered, that those who worship God through ceremonials and forms, however crude we may think them to be, are not in error. It is the journey from truth to truth, from lower truth to higher truth. Darkness is less light; evil is less good; impurity is less purity. It must always be borne in mind that we should see others with eyes of love, with sympathy, knowing that they are going along the same path we have trodden. If you are free, you must know that all will be so sooner or later, and if you are free, how can you see the impermanent? If you are really pure, how do you see the impure? For what is within, is without. We cannot see impurity without having it inside ourselves. This is one of the practical sides of Vedanta, and I hope that we shall all try to carry it into our lives. Our whole life here is to carry this into practice, but the one great point we gain is that we shall work with satisfaction and contentment, instead of with discontent and dissatisfaction, for we know that Truth is within us, we have It as our birthright, and we have only to manifest It, and make It tangible.

PRACTICAL VEDANTA

PART III

(Delivered in London, 17 November 1896)

In the Chhandogya Upanishad we read that a sage called Narada came to another called Sanatkumara, and asked him various questions, of which one was, if religion was the cause of things as they are. And Sanatkumara leads him, as it were, step by step, telling him that there is something higher than this earth, and something higher than that, and so on, till he comes to Akasha, ether. Ether is higher than light, because in the ether are the sun and the moon, lightning and the stars; in ether we live, and in ether we die. Then the question arises, if there is anything higher than that, and Sanatkumara tells him of Prana. This Prana, according to the Vedanta, is the principle of life. It is like ether, an omnipresent principle; and all motion, either in the body or anywhere else, is the work of this Prana. It is greater than Akasha, and through it everything lives. Prana is in the mother, in the father, in the sister, in the teacher, Prana is the knower.

I will read another passage, where Shvetaketu asks his father about the Truth, and the father teaches him different things, and concludes by saying, 'That which is the fine cause in all these things, of It are all these things made. That is the All, that is Truth, thou art That, O Shvetaketu.' And then he gives various examples. 'As a bee, O Shvetaketu, gathers honey from different flowers, and as the different honeys do not know that they are from various trees, and from various flowers, so all of us, having come to that Existence, know not that we have done so. Now, that which is that subtle essence, in It all that exists has its self. It is the True. It is the Self and thou, O Shvetaketu, art That.' He gives another example of the rivers running down to the ocean. 'As the rivers, when they are in the ocean, do not know that they have been various rivers, even so when we come out of that Existence, we do not know that we are That. O Shvetaketu, thou art That.' So on he goes with his teachings.

Now there are two principles of knowledge. The one principle is that we know by referring the particular to the general, and the general to the universal; and the second is that anything of which the explanation is sought is to be explained so far as possible from its own nature. Taking up the first principle, we see that all our knowledge really consists of classifications, going higher and higher. When something happens singly, we are, as it were, dissatisfied. When it can be shown that the same thing happens again and again, we are satisfied and call it law. When we find that one apple falls, we are dissatisfied; but when we find that all apples fall, we call it the law of gravitation and are satisfied. The fact is that from the particular we deduce the general.

When we want to study religion, we should apply this scientific process. The same principle also holds good here, and as a fact we find that that has been the method all through. In reading these books from which I have been translating to you, the earliest idea that I can trace is this principle of going from the particular to the general. We see how the 'bright ones' became merged into one principle; and likewise in the ideas of the cosmos we find the ancient thinkers going higher and higher — from the fine elements they go to finer and more embracing elements, and from these particulars they come to one omnipresent ether, and from that even they go to an all embracing force, or Prana; and through all this runs the principle, that one is not separate from the others. It is the very ether that exists in the higher form of Prana, or the higher form of Prana concretes, so to say, and becomes ether; and that ether becomes still grosser, and so on.

The generalisation of the Personal God is another case in point. We have seen how this generalisation was reached, and was called the sum total of all consciousness. But a difficulty arises — it is an incomplete generalisation. We take up only one side of the facts of nature, the fact of consciousness, and upon that we generalise, but the other side is left out. So, in the first place it is a defective generalisation. There is another insufficiency, and that relates to the second principle. Everything should be explained from its own nature. There may have been people who thought that every apple that fell to the ground was dragged down by a ghost, but the explanation is the law of gravitation; and although we know it is not a perfect explanation, yet it is much better than the other, because it is derived from the nature of the thing itself, while the other posits an extraneous cause. So throughout the whole range of our knowledge; the explanation which is based upon the nature of the thing itself is a scientific explanation, and an explanation which brings in an outside agent is unscientific.

So the explanation of a Personal God as the creator of the universe has to stand that test. If that God is outside of nature, having nothing to do with nature, and this nature is the outcome of the command of that God and produced from nothing, it is a very unscientific theory, and this has been the weak point of every Theistic religion throughout the ages. These two defects we find in what is generally called the theory of monotheism, the theory of a Personal God, with all the qualities of a human being multiplied very much, who, by His will, created this universe out of nothing and yet is separate from it. This leads us into two difficulties.

As we have seen, it is not a sufficient generalisation, and secondly, it is not an explanation of nature from nature. It holds that the effect is not the cause, that the cause is entirely separate from the effect. Yet all human knowledge shows that the effect is but the cause in another form. To this idea the discoveries of modern science are tending every day, and the latest theory that has been accepted on all sides is the theory of evolution, the principle of which is that the effect is but the cause in another form, a readjustment of the cause, and the cause takes the form of the effect. The theory of creation out of nothing would be laughed at by modern scientists.

Now, can religion stand these tests? If there be any religious theories which can stand these two tests, they will be acceptable to the modern mind, to the thinking mind. Any other theory which we ask the modern man to believe, on the authority of priests, or churches, or books, he is unable to accept, and the result is a hideous mass of unbelief. Even in those in whom there is an external display of belief, in their hearts there is a tremendous amount of unbelief. The rest shrink away from religion, as it were, give it up, regarding it as priestcraft only.

Religion has been reduced to a sort of national form. It is one of our very best social remnants; let it remain. But the real necessity which the grandfather of the modern man felt for it is gone; he no longer finds it satisfactory to his reason. The idea of such a Personal God, and such a creation, the idea which is generally known as monotheism in every religion, cannot hold its own any longer. In India it could not hold its own because of the Buddhists, and that was the very point where they gained their victory in ancient times. They showed that if we allow that nature is possessed of infinite power, and that nature can work out all its wants, it is simply unnecessary to insist that there is something besides nature. Even the soul is unnecessary.

The discussion about substance and qualities is very old, and you will sometimes find that the old superstition lives even at the present day. Most of you have read how, during the Middle Ages, and, I am sorry to say, even much later, this was one of the subjects of discussion, whether qualities adhered to substance, whether length, breadth, and thickness adhered to the substance which we call dead matter, whether, the substance remaining, the qualities are there or not. To this our Buddhist says, 'You have no ground for maintaining the existence of such a substance; the qualities are all that exist; you do not see beyond them.' This is just the position of most of our modern agnostics. For it is this fight of the substance and qualities that, on a higher plane, takes the form of the fight between noumenon and phenomenon. There is the phenomenal world, the universe of continuous change, and there is something behind which does not change; and this duality of existence, noumenon and phenomenon, some hold, is true, and others with better reason claim that you have no right to admit the two, for what we see, feel, and think is only the phenomenon. You have no right to assert there is anything beyond phenomenon; and there is no answer to this. The only answer we get is from the monistic theory of the Vedanta. It is true that only one exists, and that one is either phenomenon or noumenon. It is not true that there are two — something changing, and, in and through that, something which does not change; but it is the one and the same thing which appears as changing, and which is in reality unchangeable. We have come to think of the body, and mind, and soul as many, but really there is only one; and that one is appearing in all these various forms. Take the well-known illustration of the monists, the rope appearing as the snake. Some people, in the dark or through some other cause, mistake the rope for the snake, but when knowledge comes, the snake vanishes and it is found to be a rope. By this illustration we see that when the snake exists in the mind, the rope has vanished, and when the rope exists, the snake has gone. When we see phenomenon and phenomenon only, around us, the noumenon has vanished, but when we see the noumenon, the unchangeable, it naturally follows that the phenomenon has vanished. Now, we understand better the position of both the realist and the idealist. The realist sees the phenomenon only, and the idealist looks to the noumenon. For the idealist, the really genuine idealist, who has truly arrived at the power of perception, whereby he can get away from all ideas of change, for him the changeful universe has vanished, and he has the right to say it is all delusion, there is no change. The realist at the same time looks at the changeful. For him the unchangeable has vanished, and he has a right to say this is all real.

What is the outcome of this philosophy? It is that the idea of Personal God is not sufficient. We have to get to something higher, to the Impersonal idea. It is the only logical step that we can take. Not that the personal idea would be destroyed by that, not that we supply proof that the Personal God does not exist, but we must go to the Impersonal for the explanation of the personal, for the Impersonal is a much higher generalisation than the personal. The Impersonal only can be Infinite, the personal is limited. Thus we preserve the personal and do not destroy it. Often the doubt comes to us that if we arrive at the idea of the Impersonal God, the personal will be destroyed, if we arrive at the idea of the Impersonal man, the personal will be lost. But the Vedantic idea is not the destruction of the individual, but its real preservation. We cannot prove the individual by any other means but by referring to the universal, by proving that this individual is really the universal. If we think of the individual as separate from everything else in the universe, it cannot stand a minute. Such a thing never existed.

Secondly, by the application of the second principle, that the explanation of everything must come out of the nature of the thing, we are led to a still bolder idea, and one more difficult to understand. It is nothing less than this, that the Impersonal Being, our highest generalisation, is in ourselves, and we are That. 'O Shvetaketu, thou art That.' You are that Impersonal Being; that God for whom you have been searching all over the universe is all the time yourself — yourself not in the personal sense but in the Impersonal. The man we know now, the manifested, is personalised, but the reality of this is the Impersonal. To understand the personal we have to refer it to the Impersonal, the particular must be referred to the general, and that Impersonal is the Truth, the Self of man.

There will be various questions in connection with this, and I shall try to answer them as we go on. Many difficulties will arise, but first let us clearly understand the position of monism. As manifested beings we appear to be separate but our reality is one, and the less we think of ourselves as separate from that One, the better for us. The more we think of ourselves as separate from the Whole, the more miserable we become. From this monistic principle we get at the basis of ethics, and I venture to say that we cannot get any ethics from anywhere else. We know that the oldest idea of ethics was the will of some particular being or beings, but few are ready to accept that now, because it would be only a partial generalisation. The Hindus say we must not do this or that because the Vedas say so, but the Christian is not going to obey the authority of the Vedas. The Christian says you must do this and not do that because the Bible says so. That will not be binding on those who do not believe in the Bible. But we must have a theory which is large enough to take in all these various grounds. Just as there are millions of people who are ready to believe in a Personal Creator, there have also been thousands of the brightest minds in this world who felt that such ideas were not sufficient for them, and wanted something higher, and wherever religion was not broad enough to include all these minds, the result was that

the brightest minds in society were always
outside of religion; and never was this so
marked as at the present time, especially in
Europe.

To include these minds, therefore, religion
must become broad enough. Everything it
claims must be judged from the standpoint of
reason. Why religions should claim that they
are not bound to abide by the standpoint of
reason, no one knows. If one does not take the
standard of reason, there cannot be any true
judgement, even in the case of religions. One
religion may ordain something very hideous.
For instance, the Mohammedan religion
allows Mohammedans to kill all who are not
of their religion. It is clearly stated in the
Koran, 'Kill the infidels if they do not become
Mohammedans.' They must be put to fire and
sword. Now if we tell a Mohammedan that this
is wrong, he will naturally ask, 'How do you
know that? How do you know it is not good?
My book says it is.' If you say your book is
older, there will come the Buddhist, and say,
my book is much older still. Then will come
the Hindu, and say, my books are the oldest of
all. Therefore referring to books will not do.
Where is the standard by which you can
compare? You will say, look at the Sermon on
the Mount, and the Mohammedan will reply,

look at the Ethics of the Koran. The Mohammedan will say, who is the arbiter as to which is the better of the two? Neither the New Testament nor the Koran can be the arbiter in a quarrel between them. There must be some independent authority, and that cannot be any book, but something which is universal; and what is more universal than reason? It has been said that reason is not strong enough; it does not always help us to get at the Truth; many times it makes mistakes, and, therefore, the conclusion is that we must believe in the authority of a church! That was said to me by a Roman Catholic, but I could not see the logic of it. On the other hand I should say, if reason be so weak, a body of priests would be weaker, and I am not going to accept their verdict, but I will abide by my reason, because with all its weakness there is some chance of my getting at truth through it; while, by the other means, there is no such hope at all.

We should, therefore, follow reason and also sympathise with those who do not come to any sort of belief, following reason. For it is better that mankind should become atheist by following reason than blindly believe in two hundred millions of gods on the authority of anybody. What we want is progress, development, realisation. No theories ever made men higher. No amount of books can help us to become purer. The only power is in realisation, and that lies in ourselves and comes from thinking. Let men think. A clod of earth never thinks; but it remains only a lump of earth. The glory of man is that he is a thinking being. It is the nature of man to think and therein he differs from animals. I believe in reason and follow reason, having seen enough of the evils of authority, for I was born in a country where they have gone to the extreme of authority.

The Hindus believe that creation has come out of the Vedas. How do you know there is a cow? Because the word cow is in the Vedas. How do you know there is a man outside? Because the word man is there. If it had not been, there would have been no man outside. That is what they say. Authority with a vengeance! And it is not studied as I have studied it, but some of the most powerful minds have taken it up and spun out wonderful logical theories round it. They have reasoned it out, and there it stands — a whole system of philosophy; and thousands of the brightest intellects have been dedicated through thousands of years to the working out of this theory. Such has been the power of authority, and great are the dangers thereof. It stunts the growth of humanity, and we must not forget that we want growth. Even in all relative truth, more than the truth itself, we want the exercise. That is our life.

The monistic theory has this merit that it is the most rational of all the religious theories that we can conceive of. Every other theory, every conception of God which is partial and little and personal is not rational. And yet monism has this grandeur that it embraces all these partial conceptions of God as being necessary for many. Some people say that this personal explanation is irrational. But it is consoling; they want a consoling religion and we understand that it is necessary for them. The clear light of truth very few in this life can bear, much less live up to. It is necessary, therefore, that this comfortable religion should exist; it helps many souls to a better one. Small minds whose circumference is very limited and which require little things to build them up, never venture to soar high in thought. Their conceptions are very good and helpful to them, even if only of little gods and symbols. But you have to understand the Impersonal, for it is in and through that alone that these others can be explained. Take, for instance, the idea of a Personal God. A man who understands and believes in the Impersonal —

John Stuart Mill, for example — may say that a Personal God is impossible, and cannot be proved. I admit with him that a Personal God cannot be demonstrated. But He is the highest reading of the Impersonal that can be reached by the human intellect, and what else is the universe but various readings of the Absolute? It is like a book before us, and each one has brought his intellect to read it, and each one has to read it for himself. There is something which is common in the intellect of all men; therefore certain things appear to be the same to the intellect of mankind. That you and I see a chair proves that there is something common to both our minds. Suppose a being comes with another sense, he will not see the chair at all; but all beings similarly constituted will see the same things. Thus this universe itself is the Absolute, the unchangeable, the noumenon; and the phenomenon constitutes the reading thereof. For you will first find that all phenomena are finite. Every phenomenon that we can see, feel, or think of, is finite, limited by our knowledge, and the Personal God as we conceive of Him is in fact a phenomenon. The very idea of causation exists only in the phenomenal world, and God as the cause of this universe must naturally be thought of as limited, and yet He is the same

Impersonal God. This very universe, as we have seen, is the same Impersonal Being read by our intellect. Whatever is reality in the universe is that Impersonal Being, and the forms and conceptions are given to it by our intellects. Whatever is real in this table is that Being, and the table form and all other forms are given by our intellects.

Now, motion, for instance, which is a necessary adjunct of the phenomenal, cannot be predicated of the Universal. Every little bit, every atom inside the universe, is in a constant state of change and motion, but the universe as a whole is unchangeable, because motion or change is a relative thing; we can only think of something in motion in comparison with something which is not moving. There must be two things in order to understand motion. The whole mass of the universe, taken as a unit, cannot move. In regard to what will it move? It cannot be said to change. With regard to what will it change? So the whole is the Absolute; but within it every particle is in a constant state of flux and change. It is unchangeable and changeable at the same time, Impersonal and Personal in one. This is our conception of the universe, of motion and of God, and that is what is meant by 'Thou art That'. Thus we see that the Impersonal instead of doing away with the personal, the Absolute instead of pulling down the relative, only explains it to the full satisfaction of our reason and heart. The Personal God and all that exists in the universe are the same Impersonal Being seen through our minds. When we shall be rid of our minds, our little personalities, we shall become one with It. This is what is meant by 'Thou art That'. For we must know our true nature, the Absolute.

The finite, manifested man forgets his source and thinks himself to be entirely separate. We, as personalised, differentiated beings, forget our reality, and the teaching of monism is not that we shall give up these differentiations, but we must learn to understand what they are. We are in reality that Infinite Being, and our personalities represent so many channels through which this Infinite Reality is manifesting Itself; and the whole mass of changes which we call evolution is brought about by the soul trying to manifest more and more of its infinite energy. We cannot stop anywhere on this side of the Infinite; our power, and blessedness, and wisdom, cannot but grow into the Infinite. Infinite power and existence and blessedness are ours, and we have not to acquire them; they are our own, and we have only to manifest them.

This is the central idea of monism, and one that is so hard to understand. From my childhood everyone around me taught weakness; I have been told ever since I was born that I was a weak thing. It is very difficult for me now to realise my own strength, but by analysis and reasoning I gain knowledge of my own strength, I realise it. All the knowledge that we have in this world, where did it come from? It was within us. What knowledge is outside? None. Knowledge was not in matter; it was in man all the time. Nobody ever created knowledge; man brings it from within. It is lying there. The whole of that big banyan tree which covers acres of ground, was in the little seed which was, perhaps, no bigger than one eighth of a mustard seed: all that mass of energy was there confined. The gigantic intellect, we know, lies coiled up in the protoplasmic cell, and why should not the infinite energy? We know that it is so. It may seem like a paradox, but is true. Each one of us has come out of one protoplasmic cell, and all the powers we possess were coiled up there. You cannot say they came from food; for if you heap up food mountains high, what power comes out of it? The energy was there, potentially no doubt, but still there. So is infinite power in the soul of man, whether he knows it or not. Its manifestation is only a question of being conscious of it. Slowly this infinite giant is, as it were, waking up, becoming conscious of his power, and arousing himself; and with his growing consciousness, more and more of his bonds are breaking, chains are bursting asunder, and the day is sure to come when, with the full consciousness of his infinite power and wisdom, the giant will rise to his feet and stand erect. Let us all help to hasten that glorious consummation.

PRACTICAL VEDANTA

PART IV

(Delivered in London, 18 November 1896)

We have been dealing more with the universal so far. This morning I shall try to place before you the Vedantic ideas of the relation of the particular to the universal. As we have seen, in the dualistic form of Vedic doctrines, the earlier forms, there was a clearly defined particular and limited soul for every being. There have been a great many theories about this particular soul in each individual, but the main discussion was between the ancient Vedantists and the ancient Buddhists, the former believing in the individual soul as complete in itself, the latter denying *in toto* the existence of such an individual soul. As I told you the other day, it is pretty much the same discussion you have in Europe as to substance and quality, one set holding that behind the qualities there is something as substance, in which the qualities inhere; and the other denying the existence of such a substance as being unnecessary, for the qualities may live by themselves. The most ancient theory of the soul, of course, is based upon the argument of self-identity — 'I am I' — that the I of yesterday is the I of today, and the I of today will be the I of tomorrow; that in spite of all the changes that are happening to the body, I yet believe that I am the same I. This seems to have been the central argument with those who believed in a limited, and yet perfectly complete, individual soul.

On the other hand, the ancient Buddhists denied the necessity of such an assumption. They brought forward the argument that all that we know, and all that we possibly can know, are simply these changes. The positing of an unchangeable and unchanging substance is simply superfluous, and even if there were any such unchangeable thing, we could never understand it, nor should we ever be able to cognise it in any sense of the word. The same discussion you will find at the present time going on in Europe between the religionists and the idealists on the one side, and the modern positivists and agnostics on the other; one set believing there is something which does not change (of whom the latest representative is your Herbert Spencer), that we catch a glimpse of something which is unchangeable. And the other is represented by the modern Comtists and modern agnostics. Those of you who were interested a few years ago in the discussions between Herbert Spencer and Frederick Harrison might have noticed that it was the same old difficulty, the one party standing for a substance behind the changeful, and the other party denying the necessity for such an assumption. One party says we cannot conceive of changes without conceiving of something which does not change; the other party brings out the argument that this is superfluous; we can only conceive of something which is changing, and as to the unchanging, we can neither know, feel, nor sense it.

In India this great question did not find its solution in very ancient times, because we have seen that the assumption of a substance which is behind the qualities, and which is not the qualities, can never be substantiated; nay, even the argument from self-identity, from memory, — that I am the I of yesterday because I remember it, and therefore I have been a continuous something — cannot be substantiated. The other quibble that is generally put forward is a mere delusion of words. For instance, a man may take a long series of such sentences as 'I do', 'I go', 'I dream', 'I sleep', 'I move', and here you will find it claimed that the doing, going, dreaming, etc., have been changing, but what remained constant was that 'I'. As such they conclude that the 'I' is something which is constant and an individual in itself, but all these changes belong to the body. This, though apparently very convincing and clear, is based upon the mere play on words. The 'I' and the doing, going, and dreaming may be separate in black and white, but no one can separate them in his mind.

When I eat, I think of myself as eating — I am identified with eating. When I run, I and the running are not two separate things. Thus the argument from personal identity does not seem to be very strong. The other argument from memory is also weak. If the identity of my being is represented by my memory, many things which I have forgotten are lost from that identity. And we know that people under certain conditions forget their whole past. In many cases of lunacy a man will think of himself as made of glass, or as being an animal. If the existence of that man depends on memory, he has become glass, which not being the case we cannot make the identity of the Self depend on such a flimsy substance as memory. Thus we see that the soul as a limited yet complete and continuing identity cannot be established as separate from the qualities. We cannot establish a narrowed-down, limited existence to which is attached a bunch of qualities.

On the other hand, the argument of the ancient Buddhists seems to be stronger -- that we do not know, and cannot know, anything that is beyond the bunch of qualities. According to them, the soul consists of a bundle of qualities called sensations and feelings. A mass of such is what is called the soul, and this mass is continually changing.

The Advaitist theory of the soul reconciles both these positions. The position of the Advaitist is that it is true that we cannot think of the substance as separate from the qualities, we cannot think of change and not-change at the same time; it would be impossible. But the very thing which is the substance is the quality; substance and quality are not two things. It is the unchangeable that is appearing as the changeable. The unchangeable substance of the universe is not something separate from it. The noumenon is not something different from the phenomena, but it is the very noumenon which has become the phenomena. There is a soul which is unchanging, and what we call feelings and perceptions, nay, even the body, are the very soul, seen from another point of view. We have got into the habit of thinking that we have bodies and souls and so forth, but really speaking, there is only one.

When I think of myself as the body, I am only a body; it is meaningless to say I am something else. And when I think of myself as the soul, the body vanishes, and the perception of the body does not remain. None can get the perception of the Self without his perception of the body having vanished, none can get perception of the substance without his perception of the qualities having vanished.

The ancient illustration of Advaita, of the rope being taken for a snake, may elucidate the point a little more. When a man mistakes the rope for a snake, the rope has vanished, and when he takes it for a rope, the snake has vanished, and the rope only remains. The ideas of dual or treble existence come from reasoning on insufficient data, and we read them in books or hear about them, until we come under the delusion that we really have a dual perception of the soul and the body; but such a perception never really exists. The perception is either of the body or of the soul. It requires no arguments to prove it, you can verify it in your own minds.

Try to think of yourself as a soul, as a disembodied something. You will find it to be almost impossible, and those few who are able to do so will find that at the time when they realise themselves as a soul they have no idea of the body. You have heard of, or perhaps have seen, persons who on particular occasions had been in peculiar states of mind, brought about by deep meditation, self-hypnotism, hysteria, or drugs. From their experience you may gather that when they were perceiving the internal something, the external had vanished for them. This shows that whatever exists is one. That one is appearing in these various forms, and all these various forms give rise to the relation of cause and effect. The relation of cause and effect is one of evolution — the one becomes the other, and so on. Sometimes the cause vanishes, as it were, and in its place leaves the effect. If the soul is the cause of the body, the soul, as it were, vanishes for the time being, and the body remains; and when the body vanishes, the soul remains. This theory fits the arguments of the Buddhists that were levelled against the assumption of the dualism of body and soul, by denying the duality, and showing that the substance and the qualities are one and the same thing, appearing in various forms.

We have seen also that this idea of the unchangeable can be established only as regards the whole, but never as regards the part. The very idea of part comes from the idea of change or motion. Everything that is limited we can understand and know, because it is changeable; and the whole must be unchangeable, because there is no other thing besides it in relation to which change would be possible. Change is always in regard to something which does not change, or which changes relatively less.

According to Advaita, therefore, the idea of the soul as universal, unchangeable, and immortal can be demonstrated as far as possible. The difficulty would be as regards the particular. What shall we do with the old dualistic theories which have such a hold upon us, and which we have all to pass through—these beliefs in limited, little, individual souls?

We have seen that we are immortal with regard to the whole; but the difficulty is, we desire so much to be immortal as *parts* of the whole. We have seen that we are Infinite, and that that is our real individuality. But we want so much to make these little souls individual. What becomes of them when we find in our everyday experience that these little souls are individuals, with only this reservation that they are continuously growing individuals? They are the same, yet not the same. The I of yesterday is the I of today, and yet not so, it is changed somewhat. Now, by getting rid of the dualistic conception, that in the midst of all these changes there is something that does not change, and taking the most modern of conceptions, that of evolution, we find that the 'I' is a continuously changing, expanding entity.

If it be true that man is the evolution of a mollusc, the mollusc individual is the same as the man, only it has to become expanded a great deal. From mollusc to man it has been a continuous expansion towards infinity. Therefore the limited soul can be styled an individual which is continuously expanding towards the Infinite Individual. Perfect individuality will only be reached when it has reached the Infinite, but on this side of the Infinite it is a continuously changing, growing personality. One of the remarkable features of the Advaitist system of Vedanta is to harmonise the preceding systems. In many cases it helped the philosophy very much; in some cases it hurt it. Our ancient philosophers knew what you call the theory of evolution; that growth is gradual, step by step, and the recognition of this led them to harmonise all the preceding systems. Thus not one of these preceding ideas was rejected. The fault of the Buddhistic faith was that it had neither the faculty nor the perception of this continual, expansive growth, and for this reason it never even made an attempt to harmonise itself with the pre-existing steps towards the ideal. They were rejected as useless and harmful.

This tendency in religion is most harmful. A man gets a new and better idea, and then he looks back on those he has given up, and forthwith decides that they were mischievous and unnecessary. He never thinks that, however crude they may appear from his present point of view, they were very useful to him, that they were necessary for him to reach his present state, and that everyone of us has to grow in a similar fashion, living first on crude ideas, taking benefit from them, and then arriving at a higher standard. With the oldest theories, therefore, the Advaita is friendly. Dualism and all systems that had preceded it are accepted by the Advaita not in a patronising way, but with the conviction that they are true manifestations of the same truth, and that they all lead to the same conclusions as the Advaita has reached.

With blessing, and not with cursing, should be preserved all these various steps through which humanity has to pass. Therefore all these dualistic systems have never been rejected or thrown out, but have been kept intact in the Vedanta; and the dualistic conception of an individual soul, limited yet complete in itself, finds its place in the Vedanta.

According to dualism, man dies and goes to other worlds, and so forth; and these ideas are kept in the Vedanta in their entirety. For with the recognition of growth in the Advaitist system, these theories are given their proper place, by admitting that they represent only a partial view of the Truth.

From the dualistic standpoint this universe can only be looked upon as a creation of matter or force, can only be looked upon as the play of a certain will, and that will, again, can only be looked upon as separate from the universe. Thus a man from such a standpoint has to see himself as composed of a dual nature, — body and soul, and this soul, though limited, is individually complete in itself. Such a man's ideas of immortality and of the future life would necessarily accord with his idea of soul. These phases have been kept in the Vedanta, and it is, therefore, necessary for me to present to you a few of the popular ideas of dualism. According to this theory, we have a body, of course, and behind the body there is what they call a fine body. This fine body is also made of matter, only very fine. It is the receptacle of all our Karma, of all our actions and impressions, which are ready to spring up into visible forms. Every thought that we think, every deed that we do, after a certain time becomes fine, goes into seed form, so to speak, and lives in the fine body in a potential form, and after a time it emerges again and bears its results. These results condition the life of man. Thus he moulds his own life. Man is not bound by any other laws excepting those which he makes for himself. Our thoughts, our words and deeds are the threads of the net which we throw round ourselves, for good or for evil. Once we set in motion a certain power, we have to take the full consequences of it. This is the law of Karma. Behind the subtle body, lives Jiva, or the individual soul of man. There are various discussions about the form and the size of this individual soul. According to some, it is very small like an atom; according to others, it is not so small as that; according to others, it is very big and so on. This Jiva is a part of that universal substance, and it is also eternal; without beginning it is existing, and without end it will exist. It is passing through all these forms in order to manifest its real nature which is purity. Every action that retards this manifestation is called an evil action; so with thoughts. And every action and every thought that help the Jiva to expand, to manifest its real nature, is good. One theory that is held in common in India by the crudest dualists as well as by the most advanced non-dualists is that all the possibilities and powers of the soul are within it, and do not come from any external source. They are in the soul in potential form, and the whole work of life is simply directed towards manifesting those potentialities.

They have also the theory of reincarnation which says that after the dissolution of this body, the Jiva will have another, and after that has been dissolved, it will again have another, and so on, either here or in some other worlds; but this world is given the preference, as it is considered the best of all worlds for our purpose. Other worlds are conceived of as worlds where there is very little misery, but for that very reason, they argue, there is less chance of thinking of higher things there. As this world contains some happiness and a good deal of misery, the Jiva some time or other gets awakened, as it were, and thinks of freeing itself. But just as very rich persons in this world have the least chance of thinking of higher things, so the Jiva in heaven has little chance of progress, for its condition is the same as that of a rich man, only more intensified; it has a very fine body which knows no disease, and is under no necessity of eating or drinking, and all its desires are fulfilled. The Jiva lives there, having enjoyment after enjoyment, and so forgets all about its real nature. Still there are some higher worlds, where in spite of all enjoyments, its further evolution is possible. Some dualists conceive of the goal as the highest heaven, where souls will live with God for ever. They will have beautiful bodies and will know neither disease nor death, nor any other evil, and all their desires will be fulfilled. From time to time some of them will come back to this earth and take another body to teach human beings the way to God; and the great teachers of the world have been such. They were already free, and were living with God in the highest sphere; but their love and sympathy for suffering humanity was so great that they came and incarnated again to teach mankind the way to heaven.

Of course we know that the Advaita holds that this cannot be the goal or the ideal; bodilessness must be the ideal. The ideal cannot be finite. Anything short of the Infinite cannot be the ideal, and there cannot be an infinite body. That would be impossible, as body comes from limitation. There cannot be infinite thought, because thought comes from limitation. We have to go beyond the body, and beyond thought too, says the Advaita. And we have also seen that, according to Advaita, this freedom is not to be attained, it is already ours. We only forget it and deny it. Perfection is not to be attained, it is already within us. Immortality and bliss are not to be acquired, we possess them already; they have been ours all the time.

If you dare declare that you are free, free you are this moment. If you say you are bound, bound you will remain. This is what Advaita boldly declares. I have told you the ideas of the dualists. You can take whichever you like.

The highest ideal of the Vedanta is very difficult to understand, and people are always quarrelling about it, and the greatest difficulty is that when they get hold of certain ideas, they deny and fight other ideas. Take up what suits you, and let others take up what they need. If you are desirous of clinging to this little individuality, to this limited manhood, remain in it, have all these desires, and be content and pleased with them. If your experience of manhood has been very good and nice, retain it as long as you like; and you can do so, for you are the makers of your own fortunes; none can compel you to give up your manhood. You will be men as long as you like; none can prevent you. If you want to be angels, you will be angels, that is the law. But there may be others who do not want to be angels even. What right have you to think that theirs is a horrible notion? You may be frightened to lose a hundred pounds, but there may be others who would not even wink if they lost all the money they had in the world. There have been such men and still there are. Why do you dare to judge them according to your standard? You cling on to your limitations, and these little worldly ideas may be your highest ideal. You are welcome to them. It will be to you as you wish. But there are others who have seen the truth and cannot rest in these limitations, who have done with these things and want to get beyond. The world with all its enjoyments is a mere mud-puddle for them. Why do you want to bind them down to your ideas? You must get rid of this tendency once for all. Accord a place to everyone.

I once read a story about some ships that were caught in a cyclone in the South Sea Islands, and there was a picture of it in the *Illustrated London News*. All of them were wrecked except one English vessel, which weathered the storm. The picture showed the men who were going to be drowned, standing on the decks and cheering the people who were sailing through the storm.[1] Be brave and generous like that. Do not drag others down to where you are. Another foolish notion is that if we lose our little individuality, there will be no morality, no hope for humanity. As if everybody had been dying for humanity all the time! God bless you! If in every country there were two hundred men and women really wanting to do good to humanity, the millennium would come in five days. We know how we are dying for humanity! These are all tall talks, and nothing else. The history of the world shows that those who never thought of their little individuality were the greatest benefactors of the human race, and that the more men and women think of themselves, the less are they able to do for others. One is unselfishness, and the other selfishness. Clinging on to little enjoyments, and to desire the continuation and repetition of this state of things is utter selfishness. It arises not from any desire for truth, its genesis is not in kindness for other beings, but in the utter selfishness of the human heart, in the idea,

---

[1] H.M.S. Calliope and the American men-of-war at Samoa. — Ed.

'I will have everything, and do not care for anyone else.' This is as it appears to me. I would like to see more moral men in the world like some of those grand old prophets and sages of ancient times who would have given up a hundred lives if they could by so doing benefit one little animal! Talk of morality and doing good to others! Silly talk of the present time!

I would like to see moral men like Gautama Buddha, who did not believe in a Personal God or a personal soul, never asked about them, but was a perfect agnostic, and yet was ready to lay down his life for anyone, and worked all his life for the good of all, and thought only of the good of all. Well has it been said by his biographer, in describing his birth, that he was born for the good of the many, as a blessing to the many. He did not go to the forest to meditate for his own salvation; he felt that the world was burning, and that he must find a way out. 'Why is there so much misery in the world?'—was the one question that dominated his whole life. Do you think we are so moral as the Buddha?

The more selfish a man, the more immoral he is. And so also with the race. That race which is bound down to itself has been the most cruel and the most wicked in the whole

world. There has not been a religion that has
clung to this dualism more than that founded
by the Prophet of Arabia, and there has not
been a religion which has shed so much blood
and been so cruel to other men. In the Koran
there is the doctrine that a man who does not
believe these teachings should be killed; it is a
mercy to kill him! And the surest way to get to
heaven, where there are beautiful houris and
all sorts of sense-enjoyments, is by killing
these unbelievers. Think of the bloodshed
there has been in consequence of such beliefs!

In the religion of Christ there was little of
crudeness; there is very little difference
between the pure religion of Christ and that of
the Vedanta. You find there the idea of
oneness; but Christ also preached dualistic
ideas to the people in order to give them
something tangible to take hold of, to lead
them up to the highest ideal. The same
Prophet who preached, 'Our Father which art
in heaven', also preached, 'I and my Father are
one', and the same Prophet knew that through
the 'Father in heaven' lies the way to the 'I and
my Father are one'. There was only blessing
and love in the religion of Christ; but as soon
as crudeness crept in, it was degraded into
something not much better than the religion
of the Prophet of Arabia. It was crudeness

indeed—this fight for the little self, this clinging on to the 'I', not only in this life, but also in the desire for its continuance even after death. This they declare to be unselfishness; this the foundation of morality! Lord help us, if this be the foundation of morality! And strangely enough, men and women who ought to know better think all morality will be destroyed if these little selves go and stand aghast at the idea that morality can only stand upon their destruction. The watchword of all well-being, of all moral good is not 'I' but 'thou'. Who cares whether there is a heaven or a hell, who cares if there is a soul or not, who cares if there is an unchangeable or not? Here is the world, and it is full of misery. Go out into it as Buddha did, and struggle to lessen it or die in the attempt. Forget yourselves; this is the first lesson to be learnt, whether you are a theist or an atheist, whether you are an agnostic or a Vedantist, a Christian or a Mohammedan. The one lesson obvious to all is the destruction of the little self and the building up of the Real Self.

Two forces have been working side by side in parallel lines. The one says 'I', the other says 'not I'. Their manifestation is not only in man but in animals, not only in animals but in the smallest worms. The tigress that plunges her fangs into the warm blood of a human being, would give up her own life to protect her young. The most depraved man, who thinks nothing of taking the lives of his brother men will, perhaps, sacrifice himself without any hesitation to save his starving wife and children. Thus throughout creation these two forces are working side by side; where you find the one, you find the other too. The one is selfishness, the other is unselfishness. The one is acquisition, the other is renunciation. The one takes, the other gives. From the lowest to the highest, the whole universe is the playground of these two forces. It does not require any demonstration; it is obvious to all.

What right has any section of the community to base the whole work and evolution of the universe upon one of these two factors alone, upon competition and struggle? What right has it to base the whole working of the universe upon passion and fight, upon competition and struggle? That these exist we do not deny; but what right has anyone to deny the working of the other force? Can any man deny that love, this 'not I', this renunciation is the only positive power in the universe? That other is only the misguided employment of the power of love; the power of love brings competition, the real genesis of competition is in love. The real genesis of evil is in unselfishness. The creator of evil is good, and the end is also good. It is only misdirection of the power of good. A man who murders another is, perhaps, moved to do so by the love of his own child. His love has become limited to that one little baby, to the exclusion of the millions of other human beings in the universe. Yet, limited or unlimited, it is the same love.

Thus the motive power of the whole universe, in whatever way it manifests itself, is that one wonderful thing, unselfishness, renunciation, love, the real, the only living force in existence. Therefore the Vedantist insists upon that oneness. We insist upon this explanation because we cannot admit two causes of the universe. If we simply hold that by limitation the same beautiful, wonderful love appears to be evil or vile, we find the whole universe explained by the one force of love. If not, two causes of the universe have to be taken for granted, one good and the other evil, one love and the other hatred. Which is more logical? Certainly the one-force theory.

Let us now pass on to things which do not possibly belong to dualism. I cannot stay longer with the dualists, I am afraid. My idea is to show that the highest ideal of morality and unselfishness goes hand in hand with the highest metaphysical conception, and that you need not lower your conception to get ethics and morality, but, on the other hand, to reach a real basis of morality and ethics you must have the highest philosophical and scientific conceptions. Human knowledge is not antagonistic to human well-being. On the contrary, it is knowledge alone that will save us in every department of life — in knowledge is worship. The more we know the better for us. The Vedantist says, the cause of all that is apparently evil is the limitation of the unlimited. The love which gets limited into little channels and seems to be evil eventually comes out at the other end and manifests itself as God. The Vedanta also says that the cause of all this apparent evil is in ourselves. Do not blame any supernatural being, neither be hopeless and despondent, nor think we are in a place from which we can never escape unless someone comes and lends us a helping hand. That cannot be, says the Vedanta. We are like silkworms; we make the thread out of our own substance and spin the cocoon, and in course of time are imprisoned inside. But this is not for ever. In that cocoon we shall develop spiritual realisation, and like the butterfly come out free. This network of Karma we have woven around ourselves; and in our ignorance we feel as if we are bound, and weep and wail for help. But help does not come from without; it comes from within ourselves. Cry to all the gods in the universe. I cried for years, and in the end I found that I was helped. But help came from within. And I had to undo what I had done by mistake. That is the only way. I had to cut the net which I had thrown round myself, and the power to do this is within. Of this I am certain that not one aspiration, well-guided or ill-guided, in my life, has been in vain, but that I am the resultant of all my past, both good and evil. I have committed many mistakes in my life; but mark you, I am sure of this that without every one of those mistakes I should not be what I am today, and so am quite satisfied to have made them. I do not mean that you are to go home and wilfully commit mistakes; do not misunderstand me in that way. But do not mope because of the mistakes you have committed, but know that in the end all will come out straight. It cannot be otherwise, because goodness is our nature, purity is our nature, and that nature can never be destroyed. Our essential nature always remains the same.

What we are to understand is this, that what

we call mistakes or evil, we commit because we are weak, and we are weak because we are ignorant. I prefer to call them mistakes. The word sin, although originally a very good word, has got a certain flavour about it that frightens me. Who makes us ignorant? We ourselves. We put our hands over our eyes and weep that it is dark. Take the hands away and there is light; the light exists always for us, the self-effulgent nature of the human soul. Do you not hear what your modern scientific men say? What is the cause of evolution? Desire. The animal wants to do something, but does not find the environment favourable, and therefore develops a new body. Who develops it? The animal itself, its will. You have developed from the lowest amoeba. Continue to exercise your will and it will take you higher still. The will is almighty. If it is almighty, you may say, why cannot I do everything? But you are thinking only of your little self. Look back on yourselves from the state of the amoeba to the human being; who made all that? Your own will. Can you deny then that it is almighty? That which has made you come up so high can make you go higher still. What you want is character, strengthening of the will.

If I teach you, therefore, that your nature is evil, that you should go home and sit in sackcloth and ashes and weep your lives out because you took certain false steps, it will not help you, but will weaken you all the more, and I shall be showing you the road to more evil than good. If this room is full of darkness for thousands of years and you come in and begin to weep and wail, 'Oh, the darkness', will the darkness vanish? Strike a match and light comes in a moment. What good will it do you to think all your lives, 'Oh, I have done evil, I have made many mistakes'? It requires no ghost to tell us that. Bring in the light and the evil goes in a moment. Build up your character, and manifest your real nature, the Effulgent, the Resplendent, the Ever-Pure, and call It up in every one that you see. I wish that everyone of us had come to such a state that even in the vilest of human beings we could see the Real Self within, and instead of condemning them, say, 'Rise thou effulgent one, rise thou who art always pure, rise thou birthless and deathless, rise almighty, and manifest thy true nature. These little manifestations do not befit thee.' This is the highest prayer that the Advaita teaches. This is the one prayer, to remember our true nature, the God who is always within us, thinking of it always as infinite, almighty, ever-good, ever-beneficent, selfless, bereft of all limitations. And because that nature is selfless, it is strong and fearless; for only to selfishness comes fear. He who has nothing to desire for himself, whom does he fear, and what can frighten him? What fear has death for him? What fear has evil for him? So if we are Advaitists, we must think from this moment that our old self is dead and gone. The old Mr., Mrs., and Miss So-and-so are gone, they were mere superstitions, and what remains is the ever-pure, the ever-strong, the almighty, the all-knowing—that alone remains for us, and then all fear vanishes from us. Who can injure us, the omnipresent? All weakness has vanished from us, and our only work is to arouse this knowledge in our fellow-beings. We see that they too are the same pure self, only they do not know it; we must teach them, we must help them to rouse up their infinite nature. This is what I feel to be absolutely necessary all over the world. These doctrines are old, older than many mountains possibly. All truth is eternal. Truth is nobody's property; no race, no individual can lay any exclusive claim to it. Truth is the nature of all souls. Who can lay any special claim to it? But it has to be made practical, to be made simple (for the highest truths are always simple), so that it may penetrate every pore of human society, and become the property of the highest intellects and the commonest minds, of the man, woman, and child at the same time. All these ratiocinations of logic, all these bundles of metaphysics, all these theologies and ceremonies may have been good in their own time, but let us try to make things simpler and bring about the golden days when every man will be a worshipper, and the Reality in every man will be the object of worship.